National Park Explorers

BADLANDS

by Lori Dittmer

CREATIVE EDUCATION • CREATIVE PAPERBACKS

TABLE OF CONTENTS

Many animals, including bobcats, live in the Badlands.

WELCOME TO BADLANDS NATIONAL PARK!

Look at the colored layers of the **buttes**! Sharp **pinnacles** reach into the sky. Tall grasses wave in the wind.

The Badlands are in South Dakota. The area has been a national park since 1978. It covers more than 244,000 acres (98,743 ha).

★ Badlands National Park
■ South Dakota

Bighorn sheep lambs are born in late May or early June.

TRICKY TRAVEL

Early American Indians called this place "land bad." It was hard to travel across. The Badlands are known for "the Wall." This is a 60-mile (96.6 km) line of rugged rock formations.

The weather here can be extreme. It can be -40 °F (-40 °C) in the winter. It can be hotter than 100 °F (37.8 °C) in the summer.

Visiting the Badlands in winter can be beautiful but brutal.

LIFE IN THE PARK

About 60 kinds of grasses fill the plains. Some grow ankle-high. Others will reach your waist. Coneflowers and milkweed peek through the grasses.

Bison and pronghorn feed on grasses.
Prairie dogs make towns underground.
You might see them pop up to look around.
The black-footed ferret lives here, too.

A prairie dog and a goldfinch (below); a bison (right)

FINDING FOSSILS

One million people visit the park each year. Most come during the summer. Rangers take care of the park. They teach classes. They can tell you how to stay safe in the park.

You can drive through the park. Or you can hike the trails. You might find **fossils** hidden in the hills!

Mixed prairie grasses (below); eroded rock formations (right)

Dress in layers and bring water. Weather in the Badlands can change quickly!

Summer storms can produce heavy rain and lightning.

Activity

MAKE YOUR OWN SANDSTONE

Materials needed:
½ cup water
2 paper cups
2½ tablespoons Epsom salts
Spoon
½ cup dry sand

Step 1: Pour the water into a paper cup. Add the Epsom salts. Stir until most of the salt disappears.

Step 2: Put the sand in the other cup. Pour the salt mixture into the cup. Stir until the sand is wet.

Step 3: Let the mixture sit for one hour. Carefully pour off the water that has risen to the top. (You will need to repeat this step several times during the first day.)

Step 4: Leave the cup uncovered for at least one week. Tear away the paper cup. If the sides and bottom are still damp, let it sit until dry. It will feel like real sandstone! This is the type of rock that makes up the Badlands.

22

Glossary

bison — large, hairy animals native to North America and Europe

buttes — hills with steep sides and a flat top

fossils — the remains of plants or animals found in rock

pinnacles — high, pointed pieces of rock

pronghorn — deerlike animals with long, slim legs and black horns

Read More

McHugh, Erin. *National Parks: A Kid's Guide to America's Parks, Monuments, and Landmarks.* New York: Black Dog & Leventhal, 2012.

National Geographic Kids. *National Parks Guide U.S.A. Centennial Edition: The Most Amazing Sights, Scenes, and Cool Activities from Coast to Coast!* Washington, D.C.: National Geographic, 2016.

Websites

National Geographic Kids: Badlands National Park
https://kids.nationalgeographic.com/explore/nature/badlands/#Badlands-bison1.jpg
Read more about the Badlands, and take a national parks quiz.

National Park Service: Badlands National Park for Kids
https://www.nps.gov/badl/learn/kidsyouth/index.htm
Check out trail maps, learn about fossils, and find out how to become a junior ranger.

Note: Every effort has been made to ensure that the websites listed above are suitable for children, that they have educational value, and that they contain no inappropriate material. However, because of the nature of the Internet, it is impossible to guarantee that these sites will remain active indefinitely or that their contents will not be altered.

Index

Published by Creative Education and Creative Paperbacks
P.O. Box 227, Mankato, Minnesota 56002
Creative Education and Creative Paperbacks are imprints of
The Creative Company
www.thecreativecompany.us

Design by Christine Vanderbeek
Production by Dana Cheit
Art direction by Rita Marshall
Printed in the United States of America

Photographs by Alamy (Gay Bumgarner, Tom Till), Dreamstime
(Wisconsinart), Getty Images (Kick Images), iStockphoto (ablokhin,
andyKRAKOVSKI, ericfoltz, Fantastic Geographic, gkuchera,
GlobalP, gnagel, hbrizard, JohnPitcher, LarryKnupp, lightpix,
mddphoto, milehightraveler, mysticenergy, pabradyphoto, rruntsch,
studiocasper, tomolson54, Wirepec, wwing), Shutterstock (Tarchyshnik
Andrei, Big Foot Productions, Warren Metcalf)

Library of Congress Cataloging-in-Publication Data
Names: Dittmer, Lori, author. • Title: Badlands / Lori Dittmer.
Series: National park explorers. • Includes bibliographical references
and index. • *Summary*: A young explorer's introduction to South
Dakota's Badlands National Park, covering its rocky landscape, plants,
animals such as prairie dogs, and activities such as fossil hunting.
Identifiers: ISBN 978-1-64026-065-8 (hardcover) / ISBN 978-1-
62832-653-6 (pbk) / ISBN 978-1-64000-181-7 (eBook)
This title has been submitted for CIP processing under LCCN
2018938988.

CCSS: RI.1.1, 2, 3, 4, 5, 6, 7, 10; RI.2.1, 2, 3, 5, 6, 7; RI.3.1, 3, 5, 7;
RF.1.1, 3, 4; RF.2.4

First Edition HC 9 8 7 6 5 4 3 2 1
First Edition PBK 9 8 7 6 5 4 3 2 1